AF272081

Matthias Gundel

The adventures of Arie and Rike

Short stories to
smile and think about

Imprint

Bibliographic information of the German National Library:
The German National Library lists this publication in the German National Bibliography; detailed bibliographic data are available on the Internet at http://dnb.dnb.de.

© 2022/2023 Matthias Gundel

Editing and creative supervision:
Martina Gundel

Production and publishing:
BoD - Books on Demand, Norderstedt

ISBN:
978-3757-815936

Arie, Rike and the old nut trees

It was a beautiful spring morning again today. The sun was soon twinkling on the horizon and everyone wanted to enjoy the season that had just begun.

After such a long and cold winter, it was good not only for the people but also for the animals to feel the warmth and the abundant daylight. This was also the case for the stork couple Arie and Rike, who have recently taken up residence again on their vent on the vacant factory building near the former goods station. Today they were again flying through the air. They have been looking forward to their return to their now beloved domicile for a very long time.

Something indescribable had happened to Arie. The stork could not really explain it. "My wings are so light and carefrce. I feel as if I am being carried through the air by myself," the stork thought quietly to himself.

Their mutual friend, the attentive raven Rodolfo, quickly noticed the return of the two storks. Barely an hour passed before Rodolfo gave the stork couple his first visit.

In familiar company, the three of them talked about their experiences in the last few months. Rodolfo sensed that something was bothering Arie. Unlike usual, the stork made a restless impression and was not his usual calm self.

Rike, on the other hand, listened very carefully to the raven's stories and did not notice anything else about this new situation at first. However, she was also very happy and particularly enjoyed this feeling.

In an unnoticed moment, Rodolfo whispered to his friend, "If something is bothering you and you want to talk, why don't you fly a little diversions over the old walnut trees in the nearby garden?" Arie nodded unobtrusively and gladly accepted the offer.

While Rike sent her Arie to collect all kinds of material for her nest, she rested in the warm midday sun. Arie took this as a chance to visit the raven Rodolfo.

The stork could not miss the garden with the two large nut trees. This has always been a popular place to gather grass, leaves or small pieces of wood for building the nest.

Arie landed on a slightly larger branch of one of the old nut trees. What he then got to see seemed to him for a few seconds like a real rollercoaster ride between joy and curiosity.

Rodolfo was not sitting alone on the neighbouring walnut tree. "You men certainly want to be among yourselves, as I see things," spoke the raven, who was sitting next to her friend Rodolfo.

"No, no, I'm..." the stork began to stammer. "It's all right, my love. We'll do as we agreed," Rodolfo replied gently and empathetically. His girlfriend flew away and they both now had the opportunity to talk.

"What's up, Arie?" the raven asked directly, wanting to get his friend to say what was on his mind. The stork was a little uncertain at first, but then told Rodolfo in great detail. "My dear friend, I don't know how to describe it. Somehow there is an unusual tingling sensation. I fly much more easily and whenever I return to Rike, the feeling is extremely warm and comforting. So..." Arie began to tell.

At this point Rodolfo interrupted him with the words: "You are very much in love. Love is the most beautiful and precious feeling and gift in the world. You can't really put it into words. I thought so," the raven continued.

"In lo..... What?" the stork inquired, astonished and somewhat naïve. "In love! In love! Arie is in love!" Rodolfo underlined his short words. "And you: Are you in love too?" Arie asked in return.

"Of course! Didn't you see her? My dearest darling. We met here on the old nut trees in this garden. Just by chance. At first we always spent lunch together," Rodolfo enthused.

"Recently, we have been spending all our time together. Wonderful, my friend!" the raven continued. Arie was sure at this point that he felt the same way. How lucky he was to have Rike. They had both known each other for a long time, but their love was as unique as on the first day.

While both friends were philosophizing about love to themselves in the old nut trees, the raven named Rudmilla flew up the chimney to Rike. The two of them also talked about this special feeling. Rudmilla was extremely clever and could therefore also explain the uniqueness of love very well to Rike.

Deep in their thoughts and conversations, the beautiful spring day was slowly drawing to a close. Arie and Rodolfo follow together to Rike and Rudmilla. All four friends were together for a long time, sharing their indescribable happiness.

Rodolfo was known to be a raven who always found the right words for almost every occasion. So he spoke a few thoughts to his two friends and Rudmilla.

"Dear ones, enjoy it for what it is. We are sustained by love and a mutual support in life. Love makes us invulnerable. We are grateful for this experience and also for everything else that makes our lives so special."

The sun had almost disappeared on the horizon when Rike added a few words: "Let's keep our happiness and at the same time also be open to new things."

Whenever the four friends flew past the two old nut trees or settled on them, they consciously reminded themselves of the precious feeling of love that gives them a very special meaning in their existence.

Arie, Rike and the Clock of Knowledge

It was a wonderful summer evening that Arie and Rike spent together with the raven Rodolfo on their vent. After an eventful day, the three friends wanted to make themselves a delicious Italian-style dinner today. Unfortunately, however, the main ingredient was missing...

"This really isn't normal any more. Not only are the people unhappy and hectic, but there is no more pasta either," Rike fretted, thinking with Arie and Rodolfo about a sensible alternative for dinner. Unfortunately, this remained unsuccessful, but they watched the breathtaking sunset while having a cosy chat.

Finally Rike remarked: "Do you know what I find even worse? No one is interested in each other anymore. Everyone is just annoyed and I don't think anyone has even got to the bottom of it." A moment of silence followed these words.

"Maybe we should ask our cow Elsa? She always has the right answer. Who knows, then we're sure to hear a clear solution to this problem," Rodolfo the raven thought aloud to himself. His two friends immediately agreed.

They were looking forward to flying to Elsa's pasture the next day. Shortly after the crowing of the neighborhood rooster, the three of them set off, for by no stretch of the imagination did they want to lose any more time. Nowadays, time is one of the most valuable things there is and it must always be used well and sensibly. When Arie, Rike and Rodolfo arrived at the pasture, there were a lot of cows, but one was missing: their cow Elsa. There was already a clear message on the gate: "I'm off." It was written in capital letters, because unfortunately cows cannot distinguish between upper and lower case.

The three friends asked the other cows for more detailed information about Elsa's disappearance. Unfortunately, they didn't learn too much at first, until the cow Erwin gave them a decisive hint. "We have another note here from Elsa, but no idea what it means."

Rodolfo took the leaf and gently placed it on an open space in the grass. It was written there in large letters:

FOHNHAB MENIE NA NEGÜZ NOV TRHAFBA RED DNU TFNUKNA RED TIM EIW SE TIS NENOITAMROFNI NEMIEHEG HCAN.

TSI NEGNAGEG NEROLREV KRATS ZNAG ELIEWRELTTIM SAD, NEREDNA RED NEKNED NEGIDNÄTSNEGIE DNU KNHCSIGOL MED HCAN EHCUS RED FUA NIB HCI.

:NIB HCI OW, TLLOW NESSIW RHI SLLAF, EDUERF EBEIL.

Rodolfo knows through his friendship with the navi owl Antasi that the master detective Willibert Wiesel is an expert in deciphering secret messages. The raven immediately sought him out and immediately learned the translation:

DEAR JOY, IF YOU WANT TO KNOW WHERE I AM: I AM LOOKING FOR THE LOGICAL AND INDEPENDENT THINKING OF OTHERS, WHICH HAS MEANWHILE BEEN LOST TO A GREAT EXTENT.

ACCORDING TO SECRET INFORMATION, IT IS LIKE THE ARRIVAL AND DEPARTURE OF TRAINS AT A RAILWAY STATION.

No sooner had the last word been spoken than the three friends flew to the nearby railway station to continue their search for Elsa the cow. Arie, Rike and Rodolfo were more than surprised, however, when the station was empty. Not a soul was to be seen, some trains had probably been standing at the stops for days.

The only thing to be discovered were countless mice that had apparently made the railway station their new home. The three friends had the information from the master detective, but still didn't know what to do.

"So we are only at the beginning. Unfortunately, I don't speak like a mouse, otherwise I would have asked if they had seen Elsa the cow. What a stupid thing to say," Arie said, slightly exasperated.

In doing so, the stork did not notice that one of the mice no longer wanted to move away from his vicinity. Quite the opposite: the mouse gave the impression that it was listening to him attentively.

"Well, if that's all it is. I can help you very gladly, my dear guests," the mouse began to speak. Arie, Rike and Rodolfo looked at each other, puzzled, and at first didn't know what to say.

"We always thought that mice had their own language and couldn't understand us," Rike remarked very carefully. "Far wrong. Some mice have been taught your language at Mouse College. I even have the numerus mausus." replied the mouse named Oglim.

"Now out with it: Have you or have your friends seen our cow Elsa? We have an important question for her and this can't wait any longer," Arie wanted to know very precisely. The mouse Oglim looked briefly with a pointed look and moved her head slightly to the right.

Mice that move their head to the right usually have an answer to questions asked. "Of course, Elsa the cow was here earlier. She told us about the search for meaning and reason among humans," the clever mouse assured the raven and the two storks.

"And now? Where is she now?" Rike added. "Now the cow Elsa is in the big waiting room straight ahead. We were all about to go there when you showed up. Something special is supposed to happen at lunchtime, Elsa said," Oglim continued.

"So let's go!" Rodolfo urged his friends and the mouse. What happened to them then was at first impossible to put into words. In the middle of the waiting hall stood Elsa the cow and with her, in turn, an innumerable number of mice. In contrast to just now, there was a reverent silence and we all looked spellbound at the large mirror opposite the windowed entrance hall.

"There you are at last!" cried Arie with joy, wanting to fly straight at Elsa. "Shh, shh. Not now, please, my dear friends. It's nearly twelve o'clock. It's about to happen and we must not offer any interruption to the course of events." Elsa urged everyone who was in the waiting room with her.

"Life is sometimes like a waiting room," whispered Oglim the mouse to her new friends. "Sometimes you wait for something good to happen. Sometimes you wait too long and probably miss the best."

The bells of the nearby town hall rang 12 o'clock and the sun was now shining particularly clearly through the windows of the entrance door. In the mirror opposite, the light broke and then became visible.

All those present looked at the mirror as if spellbound and were able to discover an old clock dial. What was unusual was the fact that the hands moved very slowly and constantly backwards. At the top one could read: Clock of knowledge.

Of course, Elsa the cow already knew why the friends were looking for her. She herself also wanted to pursue the solution to the question of why people have given up logical and independent thinking. Elsa finally said: "My dear friends, here is the solution to your question: Perhaps you should go back into your own thoughts to find out what happened. It might also be quite helpful if you focus specifically on yourself and your behavior. Then hopefully one or the other will come to the same realization as with the clock and their thinking and actions will reinvent themselves." When Arie, Rike and Rodolfo returned contentedly to the vent that same evening, they could then catch up on their delicious dinner of pasta and tomato sauce. The mouse friends gave them enough of it from their "treasures". Hoping that the clock of knowledge would reach as many as possible, they confidently enjoyed the unique and magnificent sunset.

Arie, Rike and the broken rainbow

This summer there was a particularly frequent alternation between warm and rainy periods. The two storks Arie and Rike have experienced these weather caprices very well from their factory chimney at the old goods station.

But something was different after the heavy rain. Arie and Rike remembered that when the sun shone afterwards and the light fell accordingly, a magnificent rainbow could appear. For some time now, however, it always looked different. Reason enough to talk about it with their friend Rodolfo during an evening visit.

"Tell me, dear Rodolfo, have you perhaps also noticed that the rainbow always has an unusual coloring? One time a color is missing, then the order is different. Sometimes it doesn't light up properly either - it's all funny, isn't it?" Arie began the little discussion with the raven. "I have also wondered what it is. You are absolutely right. My feeling tells me anyway that things are not right at this time," Rodolfo confirmed the statement made.

"Do you have any idea what that could be?" Rike finally wanted to know. Rodolfo was known for having a logical and appropriate answer to almost every question. In this case, there was nothing to say and he was silent, which was quite unnatural for him as a talkative contemporary. Finally, after some thought." I can try to get the navi owl Antasi on this subject. You know that the master detective Willibert Wiesel is then also involved. He might be able to solve the problem," Rodolfo suggested, and before the two storks could give an answer, he had already flown away.

The following day, he discussed this ominous question with Antasi. The navi owl had also been appalled by the ever-changing rainbow for days. "Maybe the rainbow is broken or doesn't feel like it anymore because everyone has become pretty indifferent?" Antasi surmised and promised to talk to master detective Willibert Wiesel about it at the same time.

In his office, the two of them sat together and came to the following conclusion: "We can no longer accept this. Apparently hardly anyone has noticed or no one wants to take care of it. I know first-hand, dear Antasi, that there is an inconspicuous factory behind our local mountain. They say that not only colors for everyday use are made there, but also the rainbow. You can fly there secretly and undetected. I'm sure you'll find a clue." Willibert Wiesel urged the navigator owl.

The latter was skeptical at first because it might have been too obvious when an owl was making its rounds around the factory. After a little more persuasion, Antasi accepted the reconnaissance tour. What a sight the navi owl saw was the reason for the currently absolutely unsatisfactory situation after only a few minutes. The staff members walked haphazardly around in front of the building. Some had a loud microphone to draw attention to themselves with their words. Everyone wanted to be heard and seen somehow, but no one showed the slightest consideration for the others. Discussions and loud machine noises could also be heard from the factory building. Antasi had to calm down from the impressions and immediately started the flight back to master detective Willibert Wiesel.

"I thought so. It must have been like that for a while. Because the little factory is so hidden, it hasn't caused a stir so far," Master Wiesel remarked, scratching his pencil behind his right ear, which was known to be a sign of reflection for him.

Antasi calmed down from this experience first and continued the conversation at a later time. "Dear Master, what is to be done so that the rainbow does not remain broken? We really can't leave it like this," Antasi finally did not hesitate to remark.

"Good thinking. People often say that their hands are tied to make a difference. Here I think I will write a letter to the boss of the Rainbow Mix Factory, which you will then deliver," Willibert suggested and was sure that the navi owl would not back down on this either.

"How? I am supposed to get the situation of a possible rescue rolling. Do you have to do that?" asked Antasi meekly.

"Think about the annual award for the best navi owls. That would bring you much closer to the title this year too, and besides, it's just a letter you're supposed to file. So, go ahead and don´t be afraid of that," the master detective motivated his owl and knew that this persuasion would also bear fruit.

"All right, you're right. As soon as your lines are ready, I'll be on my way," the navi owl relented, secretly thinking of the aforementioned award that she could receive for a third year in a row. Surprisingly, it was absolutely not difficult for the master detective and he formulated few but well-considered sentences to the boss of the Rainbow Mix Factory.

Dear Mr. Many-colored,

I am sure you have already noticed that there is disagreement among the staff in your company. In no way, and with all due respect, is it my place to interfere in your company affairs. But please bear in mind that this unrest also has a great impact on the immediate and wider environment. From the rising insecurity to widespread unrest, not to mention the broken rainbow. Please give this momentary situation your full attention and do not look further and longer away. Everyone is worried about how and if things will continue. You alone certainly know the best way to go about it. I thank you from the bottom of my heart for your time and hope for a clarification of this problem in the interest of all concerned.

Kind regards

Willibert Wiesel

Antasi flew the letter to Rainbow Mixing Company shortly afterwards. Due to the continuing hustle and bustle, she had fortunately been unnoticed and was able to deposit the message in a sealed envelope in front of the building. Afterwards she informed the master detective, but also the raven Rodolfo about the current development. Rodolfo passed it on to the two friends Arie and Rike as well. Everyone hoped for an easing of the overall situation and all the more for a de-escalating effect. Antasi continued to have the task of monitoring what was happening in and around the small factory. The navi owl finally arrived back at Willibert Wiesel's house later with the pleasant news that shortly after the arrival of the letter there had been a discussion between all parties involved.

The deliberations had had their effect. The staff had spoken out calmly about all their sensitivities, worries and needs. Over time, the working atmosphere stabilized and improved noticeably. To the great joy of Arie, Rike, Rodolfo, Antasi and Willibert Wiesel, after the next downpour the rainbow was once again visible in the sky in its old and proven colorfulness. Willibert Wiesel only said at the end: "Unfortunately, it is not or only very rarely the case in real life that small impulses can have such an effect. Just a few lines do not change the world, but they can open the eyes of those who are involved in shaping it. Great steps have also started small. Let us hope and wish for the same for the current, explosive areas of life."

Antasi indeed got the award for the best navi owl again for her great efforts.

When the root men
slept through the summer

It must have been one of the first days in early autumn when the storks Arie and Rike slowly wanted to say goodbye to the winter break. This year everything was different, because nature lacked abundant rain. Reason enough to ask Rodolfo the raven about this during his visit to the large factory chimney.

"Tell me, dear friend, do you know what was the reason for the lack of water everywhere in the last few months?" Rike asked the clever raven. Usually the raven always had a logical and appropriate answer ready, but in this case

Rodolfo could only tell what his acquaintances had reported at their meeting the other day. "My dears, at our raven conference we also thought about this. I'm sure you can imagine that with so many people present, there were just as many considerations. After some back and forth, we came to the conclusion that it must have been because of the root men."

Arie and Rike looked at each other puzzled, so that even without words one could guess the big question mark above their heads.

"Sure, I'll explain to you who the root men are: These are small and inconspicuous creatures that reside in the soil and ensure that everything is kept sufficiently moist. But this year they were tired all the time. You have noticed the result: everything was very dry, for example, the grass in the gardens became relatively yellow or even dried up completely.

Arie and Rike philosophized for quite a while about the sense and nonsense of root men, until they finally came to the following conclusion: "Is there no possibility to talk to them once? I remember that they are open-minded contemporaries," Rike threw into the room.

"But you know that there is only one who can get things rolling again here. The cat Sliddus Peterle has the gift of contacting the root men and getting them to be more motivated," the raven reported.

It also turned out that humans could only achieve a short-term activity of the root males by watering. And science says: Root males inactive, no rain and no rain also brings no activity of the root males.

So it happened that the raven Rodolfo met the cat Sliddus Peterle during one of his morning flights. The two knew each other only very briefly, because the cat was not entirely at ease with the raven. In fact, the cat was a little scared because he didn't like Rodolfo always crowing loudly over him. Today it was different and Sliddus Peterle noticed that too.

The cat was walking leisurely through her little patch of forest when suddenly Rodolfo landed gently in front of her. After a few exchanges of words, finally: "We know that you talk to the root men often. Please try to convince them to become more active again. Not only have the animals, but also the people missed the green, flowering nature."

Sliddus Peterle explained that he had tried this time and again, but the root men were just too sluggish this year. He would of course continue to tackle it. What would Sliddus Peterle be if he wasn't clever and made the root males an offer? He loosened the soil so that they would have an easier job with watering. Once some of the root men were really active again, word got around among the others and the watering was assured again. The situation was much better the following year. When Rodolfo visited his friends Arie and Rike, they said: "Fortunately we managed and the problem did not become too big. With his help, Sliddus brought the root men out of their slumber and now nature is blossoming again in all its glory. The rain was then equally lacking."

Arie and Rike in search of the golden autumn

It was a glorious and warm autumn day that Arie and Rike enjoyed in the truest sense of the word on their factory chimney near the old goods station. Even at the change of seasons, there was still no question about the time for them to leave for their winter quarters in the south. The raven Rodolfo was pleased when his friends stayed a while longer, because they always have a good time together.

At dusk he visited the two storks and, how could it be otherwise, had a little question in store: "My dear ones, perhaps you have heard the word "golden autumn"? At any rate, it is often used among us ravens, but no one knows exactly what it means. Do you have any ideas?"

Arie and Rike looked no less questioning and answered the raven Rodolfo: "No concept of that. We can look for the golden autumn. It's certainly easy to find from the air. If your girlfriend Rudmilla is still with us, then we have a total of four aerial explorers."

And so it happened, and the following day the two storks and ravens made their first attempt to seek the golden autumn. They flew over a wonderfully luminous landscape. They discovered a few fields of grain and maize as well as deciduous forests in the most delicate shades of yellow, orange and red. But there was still no sign of the golden autumn. "Could it be that there is gold hidden down there somewhere that you only find at this time of year?" asked Arie to the group. But no one knew an answer. "But it is equally possible that the fruits have to be paid for in gold and are therefore quite valuable to the people," Rodolfo mused as all four of them gathered on the factory chimney from their afternoon's exploration.

After the following attempts also brought no success, they decided to ask the other animals. "Golden autumn is when the sun gives off its last warm rays before the approach of winter and everyone can enjoy it once again," said Igidius Igel, who was, however, already very pressed for time because his winter quarters had to be finished. "I think the golden autumn is connected with the wonderful colours. Look: it's a real feast for the eyes to be made aware of nature's magnificent diversity like this," explained the Freihörnchen von und zu Nadelwald, who meanwhile was busily engaged in eating a nut that had fallen from the tree. "We want to know what the golden autumn is all about. Simple. Everyone should remember that there are golden times in life, fortunately. In autumn, it's like a long holiday," the shrew philosophized, only realizing in the meantime that he would hopefully not become dessert for one of the unusual visitors.

Arie, Rike, Rodolfo and Rudmilla had now experienced very different views of the golden autumn and were able to form their own opinions about this concept. But one thing was certain: no one had to look for gold, but it is always worthwhile to rejoice in golden moments, not only in autumn.

Arie, Rike and the Chimney Sweep "Nimble Broom"

From the now traditionally inhabited chimney of the old factory complex at the abandoned goods station, Arie and Rike had a very comprehensive view of the neighboring residential area. The two were astonished when one day a man in all-black clothing checked the individual chimneys there. The two storks could in no way understand what exactly he was doing. On his top were the words "Nimble Broom".

That was all they could find out. Reason enough to ask their friend Rodolfo during his evening round. After all, he was known for having a logical answer to all questions as best he could.

"You've seen this before, dear friend?" asked Arie quite curiously as it was about the extravagant guest right at the start. "I think people need such a service once or twice a year so that their heating works again afterwards," Rodolfo explained to the two storks. "Is he coming to see us too? That would be a disaster," Rike mused. "Counter-question: has he been here before in the last few years? I think I've always taken good care of your domicile, haven't I?" the raven Rodolfo inquired kindly. A relieved shake of the head brought calm back to the briefly somewhat tense situation.

"But you know: a chimney sweep is something like a talisman for people," Rodolfo continued. "A talisman?" Rike interrupted him completely out of turn. "A talisman. It's a kind of good luck charm. If you give or receive something like that, then you symbolically wish for or receive luck."

"People and their idiosyncrasies. We storks are much simpler in our thinking. For us, having each other is the greatest happiness," Arie concluded. "Sometimes storks and humans are not so different," Rodolfo murmured as he took off for his flight to his home tree in the adjacent garden. Arie and Rike watched the setting sun with satisfaction.

Arie, Rike and the secret of the little sunflower meadow

Rodolfo and Rudmilla are both very ill, so they could not make a sightseeing flight or visit their friends on the old factory chimney. The ravens retreated to their favorite tree and tried to make the best of the situation.

The last warm rays of the sun of the light-flooded October day touched the landscape deeply as the cat Sliddus Peterle walked sadly ahead. Where there was usually joy and exuberance, the cat was really very dejected. Rodolfo and Rudmilla instructed her to pass on the message to the two storks.

"Our two friends send their apologies for not being able to come and see you. They are both ill," Sliddus called to Arie and Rike. The information affected them too, because they would have loved to spend their last late summer days with them.

Sliddus Peterle quietly and leisurely made his way back. The cat was still fascinated by a small sunflower meadow in the neighbor's garden. "Wasn't that once higher? I don't remember being able to look at such beautiful sunflowers up close," the cat muttered to herself, not sure where she had heard the soft cackle.

When she wanted to continue walking, she looked up at the flowers again. They seemed to be moving, even though there was no wind. "We are very special sunflowers because we can do magic." "Do magic how? Make everything go the way you want it to?" asked Sliddus directly. The cat was known to stop at nothing. "Yes, exactly. Why do you ask?" the conversation continued. "Well, my friends Rodolfo and Rudmilla are both very ill. We all wanted to spend a few more carefree late summer days before Arie and Rike can make their flight home to winter quarters. Can you please do something so that they get well quickly and we have a good time?" Sliddus Peterle asked.

For a moment, the cat thought she must have been mistaken after all, because the sunflowers did not yield any answers. "No, we can do magic, but we can't change the world. Sorry. By magic we mean putting a smile on people's faces and giving them a happy feeling when they look at us." "I see, that's all," said Sliddus Peterle and trotted on thoughtfully.

In the meantime, darkness fell and it became cooler. In his dream, the curious cat once again encountered the little sunflowers in the field. This time there was a different answer to his question about the recovery of Rodolfo and Rudmilla.

"Sliddus, sometimes life surprises you and unfortunately not always in a positive way. Trust that Rodolfo and Rudmilla will recover simply because they have each other. Special times also need the protection of one's own reserves in order to regain one's strength. Having important companions along the way is priceless. Believe us that recovery is not linked to pressure to succeed. The thought of the good times afterwards helps the two friends to get over this extraordinary time," the little sunflowers spoke to Sliddus Peterle gently.

A few more days went by when Rodolfo and Rudmilla were visibly better again. So Arie's,

Rike's and Sliddus Peterle's heart's desire came true after all and all friends were able to spend a carefree autumn time together.

Arie, Rike and the secret of the silver gingerbread box

It was a sun-drenched autumn day. The leaves of the trees were shining in the most delicate shades of red and one did not really want to believe that the cold season was approaching. Arie and Rike could not bring themselves to start their journey to southern climes this year either. Instead, they took Rudmilla and Rodolfo on their leisurely rounds of the local area every day.

Rodolfo was by nature a particularly curious contemporary and planned the odd spontaneous excursion while his girlfriend Rudmilla took a long nap.

That's what happened on that Tuesday afternoon. Tuesdays have always had the characteristic that surprises always happen on such days. This was also confirmed today, as Rodolfo had experienced for himself straight away.

The raven had always been attracted to the small woodland that bordered an abandoned amusement park. But it was said in the animal world that things were not right there and it was better not to go or fly there.

"What could it be?" thought Rodolfo and flew into the middle of the forest. The trees were particularly dense and the autumn sun did not manage to penetrate the density of the forest. There was also a reverent silence there.

Rodolfo landed on a rotten old tree from where he had a good view. However, the unusual atmosphere gave the raven a slightly uneasy feeling. "Maybe it would be better if I flew home again," he muttered to himself.

"But where does it go out again? This can't be happening," the raven became increasingly nervous and flew wildly around. Rodolfo was by no means an insecure contemporary, but this situation was probably not so common for him either.

While Arie and Rike enjoyed the autumn sun together with Rudmilla, Rodolfo continued to look for a way to get out of the thicket of trees into freedom. That had not been so easy, as it turned out.

During his extremely attentive flight through the dense forest, the cunning raven spotted a shiny silvery object on a small hill. Cautiously, Rodolfo landed and looked at everything very carefully.

"Do you want me to take this with me? It doesn't look that heavy. It's not big either and it's tied with a nice string," thought Rodolfo. Before he had any doubts, he wrapped the small silver box around his head. Fortunately, it didn't pull very much and the flight continued without any problems.

"Will he drift through the air on his own again?" murmured Rudmilla with a worried undertone. Arie and Rike tried to calm her down a little. Fortunately, they succeeded. What was even better, however, was the fact that they could already see Rodolfo flying towards them from a distance.

Completely out of breath and visibly excited, the raven landed with the three friends on the chimney at the old goods station. He carefully put down the silver box and tried to calm down a little.

"Is it Christmas again?" asked Arie with a slight smile, pointing to the object the raven had brought. Looking closely, one could clearly see that it had to be a gingerbread tin wrapped with a brown string.

"I think we'll open it," Arie said and tried to open the can. With Rudmilla's help, this was no problem. What came out surprised everyone. Inside the box was a shell, a small stone and three small notes.

Arie, Rike, Rodolfo and Rudmilla luckily had a good friend: Antasi the navi owl. "We have to go to Antasi right away!" they all agreed. Antasi was the one who could read and who would definitely be a great help in solving the riddle.

At the same time, everything was neatly stowed away again in the little box and all four friends went on their way to the navi owl, who was just recovering in the nearby garden from a successfully completed adventure with master detective Willibert Wiesel.

"Then let me read you what is written on the little pieces of paper, my dears," the navi owl began immediately. "This is what you should and may build on in life. Please never give it up." This thought counted towards the enclosed shell.

Antasi immediately continued with the second part: "No matter how difficult the circumstances, this is especially important. These words belonged to the small stone. This one, by the way, was very diverse in its structure, from smooth spots to corners and edges.

Finally, the navi owl read out the third little note that belonged to the string that held everything together. "Do not lose this. It is of very great importance in life." When the navi owl had finished reading aloud, everyone continued to look at each other questioningly. No one really knew what was meant by the symbols and the short sentences. Only Antasi, a master at combining and solving riddles, had the appropriate answers. "My dear friends. I think I know what is meant by all these things and messages. I would like to tell you. The shell represents trust and confidence. The stone is a symbol of strength, just like a rock. The string means to hold together or to be connected."

"And what does the find really tell us?" Rodolfo added. Arie and Rike nodded in agreement and, like Rudmilla, were eager to hear Antasi's thoughts. "Isn't it true that these are a few important characteristics that are central to all living things?" the navi owl asked.

Long silence filled the situation. Minutes seemed to pass without a single word being said or even thought. "You are right, Antasi," the four friends then spoke almost as if in chorus. "Not only should we, but also everyone else once again concentrate more on these values. Perhaps this will bring more perspective to everyone's lives."

A wonderful autumn day like this one slowly came to an end. Arie and Rike as well as Rodolfo and Rudmilla spent a little more time with Antasi. Everyone was happy about the insights and hoped that the thoughts would reach as many as possible and enrich them in the same way.

Arie and Rike save Christmas

Arie and Rike already know Christmas from last year. Once again, they decided that they wanted to experience it in their domicile in the chimney at the old railway station, despite the dark and cold season. This celebration had also transferred its very special charm to the two storks.

Of course, Rodolfo the raven was always there as her faithful companion. "There is a legend that people receive presents on Christmas Eve. Father Christmas is supposed to bring them," the raven enthused during one of his evening visits.

The storks Arie and Rike were both thrilled and surprised when they heard this. "This works in just one evening? In the whole world?" Arie curiously asked her friend Rodolfo. The raven listened attentively and was at the same time amazed that the two storks were asking such clever questions.

"But of course. It's like always: you either believe a legend or you don't. I think it has been passed on in trust to many generations. People need fixed rituals because life has become more and more difficult. All this brings a little more security and confidence," Rodolfo the raven explains with great conviction.

As we all know, winter always brings with it a lot of snow. Snow and Christmas belong together like summer and sun. But this was no longer the case and the snow had disappeared as if by magic. For a long time, the two storks Arie and Rike only knew all this from stories told by their friend Rodolfo.

Again and again, Arie and Rike asked the raven why. Rodolfo had an answer: "Everyone assumes that snow falls from thick and grey clouds when it is cold enough. Far from it, my joy. The truth is: the snow comes from a snow machine. But it's a well-kept secret," Rodolfo emphasized explicitly.

The raven continued his story: "This machine seems to have been defective for years. Sometimes it works properly, sometimes only now and then. Unfortunately, there are no repair instructions for it," Rodolfo the raven told his friends. Arie and Rike are known for their inventiveness and ingenuity, which could help solve the problem.

Even before the deepest winter was upon them, the three joys went to the hiding place where the snow machine was located. Rodolfo was one of the few animals who knew the location of the machine. The snow machine was on an ancient pear tree in the Berggold family garden.

It didn't take Arie and Rike long to realise that there were plenty of dry pear seeds tangled between the individual gears. "That was probably the little field mouse again. Plays tricks on everyone, though." With Rodolfo's help, the two storks managed to get the machine fully running again.

A short time later it began to snow. From then on, every winter there was an especially large amount of snow, to everyone's delight. From now on, no one could complain that the snow was hiding. On the contrary, everyone was happy about the white splendor that covered everything wonderfully.

December was now more than half over when the two storks received the next task from the raven Rodolfo. "I have just heard from Santa's reindeer that there are lots of presents to give out this year. Unfortunately, the hard-working helpers have dropped the lists in the heat of the preparations. Santa no longer has an overview," says the raven.

In fact, there was total despair and downright chaos in Santa's workshop. Looking closely, one could see that really no one knew their way around anymore. It was worse than a swirling anthill. It would certainly have been easier to solve any picture puzzle. A solution had to be found and pretty quickly!

Arie and Rike anxiously asked their friend: "What is to be done? Do you have any ideas, Rodolfo?" The raven only replied: "We can be an important support for Father Christmas and his helpers. I already know how." Rodolfo whispered his idea into the ears of his two friends so that no one would notice and the whole hoax would be exposed.

It must have been the night before the 4th of Advent when Rodolfo told the reindeer about his plan. In an absolutely secret mission, the storks Arie and Rike were picked up by the chief reindeer Masimus Maximus and brought to Santa's workshop. Rodolfo was not to be left out, however, and was of course there as well. The journey of the two storks was inconspicuous. Arie and Rike took their place on the reindeer's back. For once, the two had to put on their Christmas glasses so that they would not remember the way to Father Christmas. His hiding place is to remain a well-kept secret.

It is well known that storks have a keen sense when it comes to combining and organizing. For this reason, Arie and Rike quickly managed to put the countless papers with the names and gifts back into a usable system. "It's quite clear. We work according to Plan R," Arie spoke and immediately got started with Rike.

Despite the many tasks and little time, the helpers and Father Christmas went to sleep that very night. The plan was thus able to work out very well and nothing stood in the way of distributing the presents in time for the festivities. Rodolfo was, as always, particularly proud of his two friends, who returned tired to their chimney in the early morning.

"You see," said Father Christmas. "Sometimes problems solve themselves". Even though Santa did not know how this turn of events came about, he was extremely happy about it. Just in time for Christmas Eve, all the people got their presents and the celebration was saved. For the next year, the lists were then filed away in individual colorful folders and, fortunately, there was no chaos.

This success meant that Arie and Rike still had the opportunity to celebrate Christmas together with the animals in the forest. The cozy forest was located on the outskirts of the small town. For many, it was a retreat for a short break from the stressful daily routine.

The forest was also known for having the most beautiful conifers far and wide. Every year, one conifer receives an award and is then beautifully decorated and placed in the market square. The jury is always very selective and critical, because each of the trees had its own beauty and deserved a reward.

The animals in this forest have also always wanted such a great glowing tree. When Rodolfo the raven told this to his friends Arie and Rike, they didn't hesitate for long, because the time until Christmas was only a few days away. "How about we get some ornaments and make our forest shine like Christmas, too?" the two storks decided.

Rodolfo, Arie and Rike briefed the forest animals about their project at an evening meeting. Discarded glass balls were fetched from the nearby old factory. This was quite easy because they were in a huge container that was not covered. The discarded glass balls were thus put to good use.

A construction site in the city helped the animals further with the necessary lighting. "We will bring the lighting back there shortly. We just want to borrow it for the Christmas season"; Rike prudently remarked. Rodolfo made sure that despite the missing lights, everything was still adequately secured and that it was really not noticeable to anyone that the animals had borrowed something.

In the following two days, the forest animals collected all kinds of objects. The countless things were not only enough for one tree. There was so much that the whole forest could be beautifully decorated. Thus, all the forest animals enjoyed a special festive glow this Christmas. Especially Arie, Rike and Roldolfo enjoyed the carefree time with all their friends. Of course, the lighting was brought back to the construction site. Rodolfo had a plan: "We'll get things back in place on New Year's Eve. People are busy with the fireworks on that day. A few construction lights won't even be noticed when they fly through the air."

Fortunately, the plan worked out. Rodolfo the raven, as usual, had the right idea at the right time and the construction site could be fully secured again. For the forest animals as well as for the three friends, this Christmas was an unforgettable experience. They gladly remembered this unique event for a long time.

Arie, Rike and the visit of the Christmas elves

A hitherto well-kept secret in the matter of presents and wish lists at Christmas was the fact that the Christmas elves always kept a copy of their complete list in a well-hidden place. This was in the stork's nest on the old factory chimney near the former goods station. While they were there, Arie and Rike always kept a close eye on the notes so that they would not fall into the wrong hands. Only their friends Rudmilla and Rudolfo knew about this hiding place. During the summer, the Christmas elves went on an excursion together, as they always did once a year. This led them to the storks Arie and Rike, who at that moment also invited the two ravens. The Christmas elves came to the four feathered friends in a small hot air balloon and spent a few carefree hours with them. In the best manner, they accepted the ever-lengthening wish list from the Christmas elves and placed the paper under the safely built stork's nest. "Here's to you taking good care again, my dears. If we need the backup, it must be in no other place than here with you. Please remember, when you start your flight south, that the wish list really cannot be discovered in your nest. You never know, as we all know, the bad guys are lurking everywhere," the chief of the Christmas elves once again spoke urgently to Arie and Rike. They assured everyone present that they always take very good care of the writing, so that it doesn't get lost. In this year's pre-Christmas season, everything turned out differently and the Christmas elves actually lost the original wish list. Quite upset, an impromptu meeting took place. "How could this happen? We have never misplaced or lost the wish list before. The Christmas celebration is completely in danger, maybe it has to be cancelled altogether. I wouldn't even dream of seeing the sad faces of the children," the chief of the Christmas elves spoke angrily. None of the other elves had the slightest explanation for the disappearance. They were all glad that there was a copy in the nest of the storks Arie and Rike. "Let's get the replacement wish list right away, before we're too late with the preparations for Christmas," suggested the chief assistant of the Christmas elves, and the others nodded in agreement. But what had happened? In Arie and Rike's stork's nest, the copy of the wish list was not to be found. The despair among the Christmas elves grew. "Now they're gone too, and we won't make it all the way to the Deep South to ask for the copy," the Christmas elves said in horror. Sadly and with bowed heads, they all sat around the old chimney and spoke no more. Rodolfo and Rudmilla were doing their afternoon rounds when they discovered the tragedy. Immediately they took a run-up and set down in the middle of the stork's nest. "Tell me, what has happened to you?" asked Rodolfo with the utmost concern. The Christmas elves were lamenting their plight and there still seemed no way out of this more than tricky situation. Rudmilla fortunately placated the elves and steered the whole problem in another direction. "My dear friends, we can reassure you. This late summer, for once, we took the substitute wish list with us to our lair in the forest back there. Shortly after Arie and Rike left, we noticed a very curious magpie. It flew around the vent conspicuously often and seemed to be looking for something. Without further ado, we took the copy of the wish list in an overnight action," Rudmilla continued. There was visible relief on the faces of the Christmas elves, as the festivities could go on as usual. Rodolfo and Rudmilla helped them with the preparations as best they could, as the time lost in the futile search for the replacement wish list had to be made up. They were all looking forward to telling their friends Arie and Rike about this little adventure when they went back to live on their vent in the spring. If you are now wondering what the magpie has to do with all this. The answer is: everything and nothing. She has been on duty this year as a special agent to maintain the security of the replacement wish list. However, her work was far too obvious, so now she is back to her real job, which is to live happily with the animals in the forest. Rudolfo and Rudmilla have finally welcomed her joyfully as their new neighbor.

Aria, Rike and the singing stars

The period after Christmas was marked by remarkably warm temperatures this year. Instead of snow and frost, there were already the first warm rays of sunshine at the beginning of January, not to mention the beginning of birdsong. The two storks Arie and Rike had been longing for a homecoming to their domicile on the vent at the old goods station for weeks. Reason enough to take advantage of the existing weather situation to start their return there.

Rodolfo and Rudmilla were not a little pleased because they found the two friends a short time later. The town was still in a post-Christmas mood, which could be observed especially from dusk onwards due to the multi-faceted lighting of the streets and houses. "I think people are taking a bit more time with the end of the Christmas season this year, it's no wonder after the circumstances of the last few years," Rodolfo remarked during his evening visit to the chimney of the two storks. Rike had a question about this thought for the clever raven, who was about to start his flight home to Rudmilla. "Say: I heard that on the 6th of January is another holiday that people celebrate with a special custom?" she began to speak and was immediately interrupted before the actual question was finished being said. "That's right. The carol singers come on the 6th of January. But now I have to go home to Rudmilla. We want to take a little night flight over the lake, don't we? I promised her that weeks ago." Rike couldn't say anything more now, because Rodolfo had already flown away. "Tell me: carol singers? Do you know what our friend means by that?" Rike asked Arie. The stork shook his head at first and then made a guess: "We already have it good from our vent. If anyone can hear the stars sing, it's us, because we're much closer than anyone else." Rike just said, "We should get a good night's sleep now, then we can watch the spectacle completely tomorrow." The following day, there was initially no sign of the expected carol singers. "What are we going to do now? Maybe it will all start in the evening or in the darkness? What do you think?" asked Rike in a slightly disappointed voice. "Could be, could be. Where are our friends today? Maybe they've noticed something," Arie muttered to himself. Nothing special happened during the day. The storks made their usual rounds through the air and were almost a sensation for some attentive observers, as it was still far too soon for the presence of these contemporaries. As darkness fell, the first stars began to sparkle. Arie and Rike flew off in the once more, which they were otherwise not prepared to do at this time. "Do you hear anything with the stars? It could be that they are very quiet or that we are still too impatient," Arie guessed and tried to fly even higher. But Rike especially did not see the desired success either. Finally, the route went back to their vent, where Rudmilla and Rodolfo were already eagerly waiting for them. "Where and when will the singing of the stars take place?" Rike asked the two. They couldn't stop laughing, but quickly solved the riddle. "It doesn't mean that the stars are singing, but that the carol singers are out today. That is something quite different, my dear," Rodolfo explained. When he had finished explaining, a small troop of children and adults passed underneath the factory chimney. The three children were festively dressed, wearing royal robes and a crown. Rudmilla called out

to their joy: "See, these are the three carol sing-
ers. Come, let's follow them quietly and unob-
trusively, then we can definitely witness some
of their singing." The plan worked and the two
storks and ravens were delighted with the new
impressions and especially with the happy at-
mosphere that emanated from it all.

Arie, Rike and the bedtime stories of Rudolfo and Rudmilla

It was a starry night and the moonlight glit-
tered over the wide expanses of gardens and
woods that bordered the old factory building
near the goods station. The two storks Arie and
Rike found no real peace these days and were
all the more pleased when their two friends
Rudolfo and Rudmilla came to visit them.
They didn't feel much different at midnight
and were just as tired.

"What could be better at a time like this than
telling each other bedtime stories?" suggested

the raven Rodolfo. Rudmilla as well as Arie and Rike were enthusiastic about this idea. So the story hour could begin immediately.

"My dear friends, I have three little stories for you. Enjoy listening to them," the raven added and began to tell them:

What does the moon do at Christmas?

Shallow fog settled like a veil over the valley and the adjacent mountain peaks as dusk began to fall. During the day, the sun had been very kind now and then under a cloudless sky, reminiscent of glorious summer days. Due to the recurring rain, the air was wonderfully fresh, but also very cold at the same time. No wonder for the weather in mid-December at a time when hectic activity prevailed in the village in preparation for Christmas.

The only thing missing on these days was the snow, which was still a long time coming. That didn't bother the moon, because snow and moon have always not been on good terms.

While snow wanted to be everywhere and was always the center of attention when it was present, it was exactly the opposite with the moon. The latter understood his masterpiece in circling the prescribed orbit, which he liked to do again and again, day in and day out. If snow intervened, the moon became nervous because it was interrupted in its quiet way. Besides, it pleased him when he could illuminate the earth undisturbed. He was a true lighting artist and there were no limits to his creativity.

Another special characteristic of the moon was its keen perception and observation skills. Although he could not grasp everything that was happening in the world, one or two details did not remain undiscovered for him.

The moon knew from its friends, the stars, that people were always very agitated in the time before Christmas, because for many it was a very special time in the year. This was the case until the calendar page showed 24 December. As long as the moon could remember (and the moon has been around for a very long time, as we know), it always had an uneasy and somewhat sad feeling at these moments.

"I am no longer noticed at all these days. No one asks about the full moon or the other phases of the moon any more. No more moon calendar, just Advent calendar, Christmas, Christmas and Christmas," the moon grumbled to itself. When the moon became pensive, it shone much less than usual. Today this was especially the case, just at a time when joy and light-heartedness were on the agenda.

Every year on Christmas Eve, the Christmas star famously appeared, pointing the way to the manger. The Christmas star was of special elegance and importance, which the moon was also aware of. Even before the star came into use, the moon wanted to express his great wish to him and secretly hoped that it would be fulfilled by him.

Secretly and quietly, the moon took the chance to hide behind a large, dense cloud to wait for the Christmas star. There was no long wait, because the big appearance was imminent, which the Christmas star was very much looking forward to.

As if from nowhere, the moon began to speak: "Shh. One moment, please." the moon prompted the Christmas star.

"I don't have time. The world is waiting for me to remind it of the great miracle," the Christmas star replied.

"I, I, I..." the moon stuttered.

"What me?" the star inquired, getting more and more nervous as the time was really up.

"All my life I have always wanted to accompany you on your journey to the Christ Child. All this makes me curious again and again every year," the moon continued in a slightly shaky voice.

"That's alright. That's what we'll do. I could do with a bit more luminosity myself after all these years. Let's get going quickly," the poinsettia reassured the still agitated moon.

So it happened that on Christmas Eve this year the Christmas star got a companion. Not only was the star much brighter than usual, it was also rounder. People nevertheless noticed this clearly in the current prevailing disorientation. It was a special joy for everyone to look out for the Christmas star, as it gave them hope and confidence.

To top it all off, snow also joined in and there was a white Christmas. In the course of time, the moon and snow became good friends, because in addition to a moon Christmas star, the white splendor was also part of the Christmas celebration. Now we know what the moon does at Christmas and can look forward to discovering something of the special Christmas star ourselves.

The Snowman and the White Squirrel

"Dear friends, this is a successful end to our meeting this year. Thank you all for joining us and all the best until next time."

These were the closing words of the wizard and teacher Zirini, who, as every year, organized the gathering of all the white squirrels, who were now on their way home again.

By the way, white squirrels are a very special kind of squirrel because, as the name suggests, they are completely white and therefore do not always have the best camouflage in nature.

One of the visitors was the mountain white squirrel, which had chosen the old walnut tree in the immediate vicinity of a nostalgic toy shop in a small town as its home. The walnut tree offered the white squirrel a suitable hiding place and at the same time was also a suitable place to keep a close eye on the day's events, because white squirrels are curious contemporaries. During these days, it prepared itself for the approaching winter and diligently collected a sufficient supply of nuts to tide it over safely and well for the next time.

The first snowfall began as early as the end of November and was always followed by a heavy supply.

Just in time, the large shop window of the nostalgic toy shop was transformed for the following Christmas season. In addition to lovely decorations with a multitude of lights, there were plenty of toys to make every child's heart beat faster.

One surprisingly quiet late afternoon, the white squirrel dared a spontaneous, albeit brief, glance into the shop window and could hardly believe his eyes.

"This can't be true! There are squirrels on display and they are not white at all, but brown, red or black. They must have made a mistake, because squirrels are all known to be white," thought the white squirrel from the mountain and shortly afterwards scurried back into his hiding place in the old walnut tree.

The snow continued to fall heavily over the next few hours, which was reason enough for the white squirrel to spend the day comfortably in its den. You couldn't see anything anyway because the snowflakes were big and thick. It wasn't until lunchtime that the snowfall let up and the white squirrel ventured a cautious look outside. In front of the toy shop window was a snowman with a large carrot for a nose and two briquettes for eyes. In addition, a large branch adorned it to its right.

The white squirrel jumped out of his burrow onto the snowman's head and promptly got to hear the following: "Don't. That tickles. Please stop." Startled, the white squirrel took a big leap downwards onto the snow-covered ground and looked up devoutly at the snowman.

"Hello, and allow me: Snowflake of Wolkenhausen. Pleased to make your acquaintance," he said to the squirrel.

The white squirrel was taken aback and after a short while confidently replied: "White squirrel from the mountain. The pleasure is all mine."

"Thank you. Oh, a winter day like this is wonderful and I don't have to stay in Schnobi Schneebär´s snow machine."

"Schnobi, which bear? What do you mean exactly?" the white squirrel asked the snowman in amazement.

"Well, Schnobi Schneebär. Everyone knows him! Thanks to his ingenious snow machine, I am on earth and thanks to the children's joy in snow, I am a snowman," explains Schneeflokus von Wolkenhausen.

The white squirrel was preoccupied with another matter. "Tell me. Can I ask you something else?" it spoke hesitantly.

"You're welcome, go ahead. I don't know everything, but I've certainly experienced some things in my snowy life."

"I noticed that there are different squirrels on display in the shop window, all of a different color. I always thought that squirrels were white and therefore called white squirrels," the squirrel continued cheerfully.

"Well, my dear friend. I can explain that to you: Squirrels have brown, dark red or black as their main color. Only very few are born with a white color. There are countries where white squirrels are considered to be great lucky charms," explained Schneeflockus von Wolkenhausen.

The white squirrel's eyes got bigger and bigger and he was amazed.

"Does this mean that I am a very special squirrel? Please tell me everything you know about it. Tell me already!" the white squirrel urged the snowman.

The latter continued to report until he expressed the following final thought: "If you work as a lucky charm, you have an important task. A white squirrel is allowed to spread the indescribable feeling of happiness everywhere. You just have to do your usual rounds. That's enough!" explained Schneeflockus von Wolkenhausen.

When the white squirrel heard this, it felt honored and was overjoyed at the task itself.

Reason enough to be out and about as a lucky charm. The white squirrel was happy with it, as it made the people in the small town very happy.

Influenced by these impressions, it wished nothing more than that its white squirrel friends all over the world also gave everyone a happy and contented mood.

What happens to time when it passes?

Uhi Aufziehwerk was already the fourth generation to run the small watch shop and repair workshop. It was impossible to imagine the sleepy little town without his shop, as there were always customers from near and far who brought their defective watches to the master watchmaker. In the display of the shop, there were always very special clocks to marvel at, including only unique pieces and these mostly from earlier years.

Uhi himself was a middle-aged man who valued his craftsmanship and practiced it with great passion in all repair jobs.

The time between the years was particularly busy. Here, numerous people had the opportunity to tidy up and clear out, and as chance would have it, they often found defective clocks that were too good to dispose of.

Uhi Aufziehwerk was happy about the tasks that distracted him from his pensiveness especially in these days. Between Christmas and

New Year's Eve, the hours were often filled with melancholy for him, as it was precisely here that he became aware of how quickly a year could pass and how much one had either lost time or spent senselessly.

Recently, a strange customer visited him, bringing with him an unusual watch. It was a mechanical pocket watch that had no dial.

Uhi deliberately asked: "You are sure you only want me to repair the movement? After all, the crucial part of your watch is missing, namely the dial."

The customer, named Bene Klingel, replied briefly: "No, no, that's all right. I don't need the dial. Don't be surprised. When can I pick up the watch again?"

"I'll definitely be done with it in a few days. It won't cost too much either, because I have all the spare parts in stock," Uhi Aufziehwerk explained and was glad that this contemporary had left his shop again. It was a little strange to him because the customer, wearing a completely green suit and green sunglasses, had also left a distant impression.

Uhi set to work that same day, because the weather was anything but inviting and what's better on a grey and dreary day than fixing other people's clocks?

"Somehow the lid doesn't open properly," Uhi Aufziehwerk muttered to himself, desperately searching for another and more suitable tool. He could hardly believe his eyes when the lid was finally open and there was a small piece of paper behind it. Gently he unfolded the piece of paper and began to read: "What happens to time when it passes?" There was nothing more in the way of information. Uhi was very surprised to read such a message and did not know for the life of him whether he should inform Mr. Klingel about the strange find immediately.

Master Aufziehwerk went about his work and kept looking at the enclosed note. He didn't have an answer to this question either, although he had asked himself it several times. "What is supposed to happen with the time? I don't know. It's not infinite, as we know," he grumbled to himself and put the finished pocket watch on the worktable without any dials.

The following night, Uhi had a strange dream. He was standing on a shore and in front of him was a huge ocean. As luck would have it, the question from the clock came back to him just now. Suddenly, an old fisherman's wife appeared beside him. "You want to know what happens to time when it passes. Time is like the ocean. Sometimes it comes and sometimes it goes, like the ripples. When it disappears, it becomes one with the water and brings forth the most marvelous sea creatures and sea plants. Time is not unlimited, but only those who use it properly can bear fruit from it." These were the thoughts of the fisherman's wife, who disappeared again without waiting for a reaction from Uhi.

Two more nights followed, which the master Aufziehwerk spent with more dreams. Over and over again, it was about the question he had found on the note in Bene Klingel's watch. In his dream today, he was standing in front of a huge mountain range whose peaks were all covered with snow. Here he met an old shepherd who was about to lead his sheep to pasture.

"If you wonder what happens to time when it passes, let me give you an answer. Time retreats to the top of the mountains. There it will rest because people have forgotten how to use it wisely. People have many rash thoughts, which quickly turn into bad habits or even evil actions, both large and small. Time keeps giving people new opportunities, but they often remain unused or without the necessary insight to rethink."

On the third night, Uhi found himself in front of a large forest. At the meeting of a dwarf family, the question was once again what happens to time when it passes.

"My dear friend, time is moving into the forest here. After all, the forest is the epitome of an end and a new beginning at the same time. Trees come into being, grow, grow older and finally find their rest. Never forget that time is a special gift that is given to you. Not every time is good, but every time always holds experiences for you. These, along with your memories of carefree days, are an important part of your life. No matter how difficult and hopeless a phase of life is, try to go on anyway. Just like the forest, because it never gives up!"

With these thoughts, the dwarf family left the master watchmaker Uhi again and he awoke from his dream.

Today was the day to change into the New Year and opportunity enough to think about the meaningful use of the given time. Uhi

Aufziehwerk opened Bene Klingel's pocket watch again for the New Year and added a second handwritten note with the following sentence:

> *Time does not pass, it*
> *always comes back*
> *to you.*
> *Accept this precious gift*
> *and make something of it.*

Acknowledgement

With all my heart I thank my beloved wife Martina for the ideas, the editing and especially for the lovely cover picture for the short stories of the two sturgeons Arie and Rike.